THE FUNNY SIDE

THE FUNNY SIDE
101 Humorous Poems

Edited
with an introduction by
WENDY COPE

faber and faber

First published in 1998
by Faber and Faber Limited
Bloomsbury House, 74–77 Great Russell Street,
London, WC1B 3DA
This paperback edition first published in 2012

Typeset by Faber and Faber Ltd
Printed and bound by CPI Group (UK) Ltd, Croydon, CRO 4YY

A CIP record for this book
is available from the British Library

ISBN 978-0-571-28815-1

2 4 6 8 10 9 7 5 3 1

Contents

Introduction

I was halfway through compiling this anthology when a letter arrived from a friend. 'My guess is', it said, 'that your major task will be writing the preface – defining comic verse, distinguishing it from satiric verse, providing a definition of light verse, etc.' My heart sank. Defining light verse – along with eating haggis for a second time, climbing Mount Everest, and reading the telephone book from cover to cover – is on the list of things I definitely do not want to do in life.

It didn't take long to decide that, whatever anybody expected, I wasn't going to write an essay about definitions. Anyway, this isn't an anthology of light verse, it is a book of funny poems. If anyone needs me to define 'funny', or 'humorous', they have my sympathy.

As for 'light verse', I greatly dislike the term. I don't believe it is useful any more, and I wish we could scrap it. The word 'light' seems to imply that a poem can't be funny and serious (weighty) at the same time. Some people do believe that a humorous poem can't be deeply felt, or deal with anything that matters very much. In fact, much humorous writing arises from despair and misery. In this book you will find poems about being broken-hearted, about obsessive love, about dissatisfaction with a marriage or a life, and about feeling suicidal. Experience has taught me that genuinely funny poems on such subjects can be enormously helpful at some of the darkest moments of one's life. Funny writing – not just in poems but in novels, articles and television and radio programmes – has saved my sanity on many occasions. I am at a loss to understand why it is considered less important than unfunny writing.

Of course, not all the poems in this book deal with the stuff of emotional crisis. One (by Gavin Ewart) will cheer you up if you have to waste your life at tedious meetings. Julie O'Callaghan's poem about theories of management should help a few employees through another week. Those women readers (an estimated 100 per cent) who sometimes find themselves patronised by men may feel better for meeting Simon Armitage's appalling garage mechanic. These, too, are subjects that matter, and the poets use their sense of humour to good effect in dealing with them.

However, in pointing out the seriousness of some of these poems, I have no wish to disparage the spirit of playfulness that is also much in evidence. Playfulness is an important and valuable element in poetry. Some poems here – such as Harry Graham's 'Poetical Economy' or Lewis Carroll's 'The Mad Gardener's Song' – are pure play. These, I admit, could sensibly be described as light verse. Carroll's poem also belongs in another category: nonsense verse. Most nonsense verse bores me – this is one of the exceptions.

The other Carroll poem, 'Poeta Fit, Non Nascitur', pours scorn on the power of poetic fashion. Even though poetic fashion has changed since Lewis Carroll's time (it changes every ten years or so), I still find the poem very funny and very much to the point. I have tried not to include too many items about poetry and poets but I'm not sure I've succeeded. There are only a few that depend on knowledge of particular works of literature and, in each case, the work is very well-known.

One decision I had to make concerned unintentionally

funny poems. Was I going to include poor old McGonagall? I left him aside and in the end couldn't find room for him. I wouldn't have dared to ask for permission to include unintentionally funny poems by authors who are still in copyright, although I did briefly wonder about Simon Rae's 'Ode to a Goal'. It makes me laugh, but I know that Simon is seriously enthusiastic about such things. He assures me it is meant to be funny, and I believe him.

If I had been asked to edit The Faber Book of Funny Poems, or of Light Verse or anything else, I would probably have refused. This is a personal selection of poems that amuse me. Some I had known (and been reciting) for years. Some are rediscoveries, and some new to me. The only constraint was that there had to be 101 poems. I've counted 'Three Riddled Riddles' as one poem, and done the same with Strugnell's three haiku. This should help to make up for the fact that some of the poems are very short, and that one, by Don Paterson, is wordless.

Several friends and acquaintances suggested poems I might look at, or helped in other ways. My thanks to Jane Feaver, Sophie Hannah, Jeremy Kingston, Simon Rae, Morag Styles, N. S. Thompson and Clive Wilmer. Also to Sheila Burns and Suzi Rae, and to the staffs of Moberly Library at Winchester College, the South Bank Poetry Library, and the Winchester bookshop P & G Wells. Christopher Reid, the poetry editor at Faber, has been helpful beyond the call of duty.

Most of all I must thank Lachlan Mackinnon, a walking encyclopaedia of literature, for his advice and patience. I am sorry that I have had to disappoint him over one poem he was keen to see included. This is the obscene limerick beginning 'There was a young man of Madras'. When he first suggested it, I asked how it went, listened, and said no. A few days later he asked if I knew that Jean-Paul Sartre had written a funny poem.

'Really?' I responded eagerly. 'Can you get hold of a copy?'

'It goes like this,' he said. 'Il y avait un jeune homme de Madras...'

When he 'remembered' that Mao Tse Tung had composed some comic verse, I knew exactly what to expect – some Chinese-sounding syllables followed by the name of a certain city in India. He also 'found' me an amusing poem by E. E. Cummings:

> therewasonceayoung
> man
> (of Madras) whose

There's more, but I'm not going to quote it.

Wendy Cope
May 1998

THE FUNNY SIDE

Money

That money talks
I won't deny.
I heard it once,
It said, 'Goodbye.'

Fatigue

I'm tired of Love: I'm still more tired of Rhyme.
But Money gives me pleasure all the time.

Strike among the Poets

In his chamber, weak and dying,
    While the Norman baron lay,
Loud, without, his men were crying
    'Shorter hours and better pay.'

Know you why the ploughman, fretting,
    Homeward plods his weary way
Ere his time? He's after getting
    Shorter hours and better pay.

See! the *Hesperus* is swinging
    Idle in the wintry bay,
And the skipper's daughter's singing
    'Shorter hours and better pay.'

Where's the Minstrel Boy? I've found him
    Joining in the labour fray
With his placards slung around him,
    'Shorter hours and better pay.'

Oh, young Lochinvar is coming;
    Though his hair is getting grey,
Yet I'm glad to hear him humming
    'Shorter hours and better pay.'

E'en the Boy upon the Burning
    Deck has got a word to say,
Something rather cross concerning
    Shorter hours and better pay.

Lives of great men all remind us
    We can make as much as they,
Work no more, until they find us
    Shorter hours and better pay.

Poetical Economy

What hours I spent of precious time,
   What pints of ink I used to waste,
Attempting to secure a rhyme
   To suit the public taste,
Until I found a simple plan
Which makes the lamest lyric scan!

When I've a syllable de trop,
   I cut it off, without apol.:
This verbal sacrifice, I know,
   May irritate the schol.;
But all must praise my dev'lish cunn.
Who realize that Time is Mon.

My sense remains as clear as cryst.,
   My style as pure as any Duch.
Who does not boast a bar sinist.
   Upon her fam. escutch.;
And I can treat with scornful pit.
The sneers of ev'ry captious crit.

I gladly publish to the pop.
   A scheme of which I make no myst.,
And beg my fellow scribes to cop.
   This-labour-saving syst.
I offer it to the consid.
Of ev'ry thoughtful individ.

The author, working like a beav.,
  His readers' pleasure could redoub.
Did he but now and then abbrev.
  The work he gives his pub.
(This view I most partic. suggest
To A. C. Bens. and G. K. Chest.)

If Mr Caine rewrote The Scape.,
  And Miss Correll condensed Barabb.,
What could they save in foolscap pape.
  Did they but cult. the hab.,
Which teaches people to suppress
All syllables that are unnec.!

If playwrights would but thus dimin.
  The length of time each drama takes,
(The Second Mrs Tanq. by Pin.
  Or even Ham., by Shakes.)
We could maintain a watchful att.
When at a Mat. on Wed. or Sat.

Have done, ye bards, with dull monot.!
  Foll. my examp., O, Stephen Phill.,
O, Owen Seam., O, William Wat.,
  O, Ella Wheeler Wil.,
And share with me the grave respons.
Of writing this amazing nons.!

A Ballad of Abbreviations

The American's a hustler, for he says so,
    And surely the American must know.
He will prove to you with figures why it pays so
    Beginning with his boyhood long ago.
When the slow-maturing anecdote is ripest,
    He'll dictate it like a Board of Trade Report,
And because he has no time to call a typist,
    He calls her a Stenographer for short.

He is never known to loiter or malinger,
    He rushes, for he knows he has 'a date';
He is always on the spot and full of ginger,
    Which is why he is invariably late.
When he guesses that it's getting even later,
    His vocabulary's vehement and swift,
And he yells for what he calls the Elevator,
    A slang abbreviation for a lift.

Then nothing can be nattier or nicer
    For those who like a light and rapid style
Than to trifle with a work of Mr Dreiser
    As it comes along in waggons by the mile.
He has taught us what a swift selective art meant
    By description of his dinners and all that,
And his dwelling, which he says is an Apartment,
    Because he cannot stop to say a flat.

We may whisper of his wild precipitation,
    That its speed is rather longer than a span,
But there really is a definite occasion
    When he does not use the longest word he can.
When he substitutes, I freely make admission,
    One shorter and much easier to spell;
If you ask him what he thinks of Prohibition,
    He may tell you quite succinctly it is Hell.

ANONYMOUS

Liquor and Longevity

The horse and mule live thirty years
And nothing know of wines and beers.
The goat and sheep at twenty die
And never taste of Scotch or Rye.
The cow drinks water by the ton
And at eighteen is mostly done.
The dog at fifteen cashes in
Without the aid of rum and gin.
The cat in milk and water soaks
And then in twelve short years it croaks.
The modest, sober, bone-dry hen
Lays eggs for nogs, then dies at ten.
All animals are strictly dry:
They sinless live and swiftly die;
But sinful, ginful rum-soaked men
Survive for three score years and ten.
And some of them, a very few,
Stay pickled till they're ninety-two.

Ballade of Soporific Absorption

Ho! Ho! Yes! Yes! It's very all well,
   You may drunk I am think, but I tell you I'm not,
I'm as sound as a fiddle and fit as a bell,
   And stable quite ill to see what's what.
   I under *do* stand you surprise a got
When I headed my smear with gooseberry jam:
   And I've swallowed, I grant, a beer of lot –
But I'm not so think as you drunk I am.

Can I liquor my stand? Why, yes, like hell!
   I care not how many a tossed I've pot,
I shall stralk quite weight and not yutter an ell,
   My feech will not spalter the least little jot:
   If you knownly had own! – well, I gave him a dot,
And I said to him, 'Sergeant, I'll come like a lamb –
   The floor it seems like a storm in a yacht,
But I'm not so think as you drunk I am.'

For example, to prove it I'll tale you a tell –
   I once knew a fellow named Apricot –
I'm sorry, I just chair over a fell –
   A trifle – this chap, on a very day hot –
   If I hadn't consumed that last whisky of tot! –
As I said now, this fellow, called Abraham –
   Ah? One more? Since it's you! Just a do me will spot –
But I'm not so think as you drunk I am.

ENVOI

So, Prince, you suggest I've bolted my shot?
Well, like what you say, and soul your damn!
I'm an upple litset by the talk you rot –
But I'm not so think as you drunk I am.

Life on Earth

When he came in
she gave him a flower
called 'Welcome Home Husband
However Drunk You Be'.
I am not drunk, he said;
this is not my home,
I am not your husband.

'Three mistakes
do not change the name of a flower'
she replied.

Portrait of the Artist
as a Prematurely Old Man

It is common knowledge to every schoolboy and even
  every Bachelor of Arts
That all sin is divided into two parts.
One kind of sin is called a sin of commission, and that is
  very important,
And it is what you are doing when you are doing
  something you ortant,
And the other kind of sin is just the opposite and is called a
  sin of omission and is equally bad in the eyes of all
  right-thinking people, from Billy Sunday to Buddha,
And it consists of not having done something you shuddha.
I might as well give you my opinion of these two kinds of
  sin as long as, in a way, against each other we are pitting
  them,
And that is, don't bother your head about sins of
  commission because however sinful, they must at least
  be fun or else you wouldn't be committing them.
It is the sin of omission, the second kind of sin,
That lays eggs under your skin.
The way you get really painfully bitten
Is by the insurance you haven't taken out and the checks
  you haven't added up the stubs of and the appointments
  you haven't kept and the bills you haven't paid and the
  letters you haven't written.
Also, about sins of omission there is one particularly
  painful lack of beauty,
Namely, it isn't as though it had been a riotous red-letter
  day or night every time you neglected to do your duty;

You didn't get a wicked forbidden thrill
Every time you let a policy lapse or forgot to pay a bill;
You didn't slap the lads in the tavern on the back and loudly
    cry Whee,
Let's all fail to write just one more letter before we go home,
    and this round of unwritten letters is on me.
No, you never get any fun
Out of the things you haven't done,
But they are the things that I do not like to be amid,
Because the suitable things you didn't do give you a lot
    more trouble than the unsuitable things you did.
The moral is that it is probably better not to sin at all, but if
    some kind of sin you must be pursuing,
Well, remember to do it by doing rather than by not doing.

ANONYMOUS

The Village Burglar

Under the spreading gooseberry bush
  The village burglar lies;
The burglar is a hairy man
  With whiskers round his eyes.

He goes to church on Sundays;
  He hears the Parson shout;
He puts a penny in the plate
  And takes a shilling out.

The Sergeant's Song
(from The Pirates of Penzance*)*

When a felon's not engaged in his employment (His
    employment) –
Or maturing his felonious little plans (Little plans) –
His capacity for innocent enjoyment ('Cent enjoyment) –
Is just as great as any honest man's (Honest man's) –
Our feelings we with difficulty smother ('Culty smother) –
When constabulary duty's to be done (To be done) –
Ah, take one consideration with another (With another) –
A policeman's lot is not a happy one.

When the enterprising burglar's not a-burgling (Not
    a-burgling) –
When the cut-throat isn't occupied in crime ('Pied in
    crime) –
He loves to hear the little brook a-gurgling (Brook
    a-gurgling) –
And listen to the merry village chime (Village chime) –
When the coster's finished jumping on his mother (On his
    mother) –
He loves to lie a-basking in the sun (In the sun) –
Ah, take one consideration with another (With another) –
A policeman's lot is not a happy one.

The Ruined Maid

'O 'Melia, my dear, this does everything crown!
Who could have supposed I should meet you in Town?
And whence such fair garments, such prosperi-ty?' –
'O didn't you know I'd been ruined?' said she.

– 'You left us in tatters, without shoes or socks,
Tired of digging potatoes, and spudding up docks;
And now you've gay bracelets and bright feathers three!' –
'Yes: that's how we dress when we're ruined,' said she.

– 'At home in the barton you said "thee" and "thou",
And "thik oon", and "theäs oon", and "t'other"; but now
Your talking quite fits 'ee for high compa-ny!' –
'Some polish is gained with one's ruin,' said she.

– 'Your hands were like paws then, your face blue and bleak
But now I'm bewitched by your delicate cheek,
And your little gloves fit as on any la-dy!'
'We never do work when we're ruined,' said she.

– 'You used to call home-life a hag-ridden dream,
And you'd sigh, and you'd sock; but at present you seem
To know not of megrims or melancho-ly!' –
'True. One's pretty lively when ruined,' said she.

– 'I wish I had feathers, a fine sweeping gown,
And a delicate face, and could strut about Town!' –
'My dear – a raw country girl, such as you be,
Cannot quite expect that. You ain't ruined,' said she.

If People Disapprove of You

Make being disapproved of your hobby.
Make being disapproved of your aim.
Devise new ways of scoring points
In the Being Disapproved Of Game.

Let them disapprove in their dozens.
Let them disapprove in their hordes.
You'll find that being disapproved of
Builds character, brings rewards

Just like any form of striving.
Don't be arrogant; don't coast
On your high disapproval rating.
Try to be disapproved of most.

At this point, if it's useful,
Draw a pie-chart or a graph.
Show it to someone who disapproves.
When they disapprove, just laugh.

Count the emotions you provoke:
Anger, suspicion, shock.
One point for each of these and two
For every boat you rock.

Feel yourself warming to your task –
You do it bloody well.
At last you've found an area
In which you can excel.

Savour the thrill of risk without
The fear of getting caught.
Whether they sulk or scream or pout,
Enjoy your new-found sport.

Meanwhile all those who disapprove
While you are having fun
Won't even know your game exists
So tell yourself you've won.

To a Lady with 'The Temple of Fame'

What's Fame with Men, by Custom of the Nation,
Is call'd in Women only Reputation:
About them both why keep we such a pother?
Part you with one, and I'll renounce the other.

A Joke Versified

'Come, come,' said Tom's father, 'at your time of life,
    There's no longer excuse for thus playing the rake –
It is time you should think, boy, of taking a wife.' –
    'Why so it is, father, – whose wife shall I take?'

Autumn

He told his life story to Mrs Courtly
Who was a widow. 'Let us get married shortly,'
He said. 'I am no longer passionate,
But we can have some conversation before it is too late.'

The Best of Husbands
(Imitated from the German)

Oh, I have a husband as good as can be;
No woman could wish for a better than he!
Sometimes, indeed, he may chance to be wrong,
But his love for me is uncommonly strong!

He has one little fault that makes me fret,
He has always less money, by far, than debt;
Moreover, he thrashes me, now and then, –
But, excepting that, he's the best of men!

I own he is dreadfully given to drink;
And besides he is rather too fond, I think,
Of playing at cards and dice; but then,
Excepting that, he's the best of men!

He loves to chat with the girls, I know
('Tis the way with the men, – they're always so), –
But what care I for his flirting, when,
Excepting that, he's the best of men!

I can't but say I think he is rash
To pawn my pewter, and spend the cash;
But how can I scold my darling, when,
Excepting that, he's the best of men?

When soak'd with tipple, he's hardly polite,
But knocks the crockery left and right,
And pulls my hair, and growls again;
But, excepting that, he's the best of men!

Yes, such is the loyalty I have shown;
But I have a spouse who is all my own;
As good, indeed, as a man can be,
And who could ask for a better than he?

Sonnet

Oh, oh, you will be sorry for that word!
Give back my book and take my kiss instead.
Was it my enemy or my friend I heard,
'What a big book for such a little head!'
Come, I will show you now my newest hat,
And you may watch me purse my mouth and prink!
Oh, I shall love you still, and all of that.
I never again shall tell you what I think.
I shall be sweet and crafty, soft and sly;
You will not catch me reading any more:
I shall be called a wife to pattern by;
And some day when you knock and push the door,
Some sane day, not too bright and not too stormy,
I shall be gone, and you may whistle for me.

ALMA DENNY

Mrs Hobson's Choice

What shall a woman
Do with her ego,
Faced with the choice
That it go or he go?

from Shorts

To the man-in-the-street, who, I'm sorry to say
    Is a keen observer of life,
The word Intellectual suggests straight away
    A man who's untrue to his wife.

Love Song

My own dear love, he is strong and bold
    And he cares not what comes after.
His words ring sweet as a chime of gold,
    And his eyes are lit with laughter.
He is jubilant as a flag unfurled –
    Oh, a girl, she'd not forget him.
My own dear love, he is all my world –
    And I wish I'd never met him.

My love, he's mad, and my love, he's fleet,
    And a wild young wood-thing bore him!
The ways are fair to his roaming feet,
    And the skies are sunlit for him.
As sharply sweet to my heart he seems
    As the fragrance of acacia.
My own dear love, he is all my dreams –
    And I wish he were in Asia.

My love runs by like a day in June,
    And he makes no friends of sorrows.
He'll tread his galloping rigadoon
    In the pathway of the morrows.
He'll live his days where the sunbeams start,
    Nor could storm or wind uproot him.
My own dear love, he is all my heart –
    And I wish somebody'd shoot him.

One-Track Mind

Why does she take unnecessary trips?
She lives just opposite a row of shops.
She went to Crewe to buy a bag of chips.
She went to Birmingham to buy lamb chops.

She has no time for aeroplanes or boats.
She cannot get enough of British Rail.
She went to Liverpool for Quaker Oats
Then Halifax to buy the *Daily Mail*.

She went to Chester for a pair of tights.
Every weekend she's up and down some track.
She went to York for twenty Marlboro Lights.
She went to Stalybridge and came straight back.

Once, on her way to Hull for cottage cheese,
She saw him. All he said was *Tickets, please.*

Dewpond and Black Drainpipes

In order to distract me, my mother
sent me on an Archaeology Week.
We lived in tents on the downs,
and walked over to the site
every morning. It was an old dewpond.

There was a boy there called Charlie.
He was the first boy I had really met.
I was too shy to go to the pub,
but I hung around the camp every night
waiting for him to come back.

He took no notice of me at first,
but one night the two of us
were on Washing-Up together.
I was dressed in a black jersey
and black drainpipes, I remember.

You in mourning? he said.
He didn't know I was
one of the first beatniks.
He put a drying-up cloth
over my head and kissed me

through the linen Breeds Of Dogs.
I love you, Charlie I said.
Later, my mother blamed herself
for what had happened. *The Romans
didn't even interest her*, she said.

Siren Song

This is the one song everyone
would like to learn: the song
that is irresistible:

the song that forces men
to leap overboard in squadrons
even though they see the beached skulls

the song nobody knows
because anyone who has heard it
is dead, and the others can't remember.

Shall I tell you the secret
and if I do, will you get me
out of this bird suit?

I don't enjoy it here
squatting on this island
looking picturesque and mythical

with these two feathery maniacs,
I don't enjoy singing
this trio, fatal and valuable.

I will tell the secret to you,
to you, only to you.
Come closer. This song

is a cry for help: Help me!
Only you, only you can,
you are unique

at last. Alas
it is a boring song
but it works every time.

GAVIN EWART

The Lover Writes a One-Word Poem

You!

DON PATERSON

On Going to Meet a Zen Master in the Kyushu Mountains and Not Finding Him

for A.G.

Strugnell's Haiku

(i)

The cherry blossom
In my neighbour's garden – Oh!
It looks really nice.

(ii)

The leaves have fallen
And the snow has fallen and
Soon my hair also . . .

(iii)

November evening:
The moon is up, rooks settle,
The pubs are open.

There Was a Young Bard of Japan

There was a young bard of Japan,
Whose limericks never would scan;
    When told it was so,
    He said: 'Yes, I know,
But I always try and get as many words into the last line as
    I possibly can.'

A Tale of Two Metres

I heard a little couplet cry:
'Will God or Someone tell me why
We couplets are condemned to squeeze
Our wisdom into shapes like these?
To speak with gravity and treat
Of higher truths one needs more feet:
Four will not do! Four are too few.
Five feet for me or I am through!'

Not only I but Poesy had heard:
She raised her sceptre, uttered not a word,
But struck the couplet dead. And what do you think?
Its ashes stirred – and formed, in living ink,
A couplet calm as Zeno and as stoic –
The couplet known to fame as The Heroic.

Once

*Verse in the 20th century has largely escaped
the straitjacket of traditional metrics.*
The Oxford Companion to English Literature, fifth edn.

Once, to a woman and a man,
Poets wrote stuff that you could scan.

Straitjacketed to rules, they thus
Produced verse risible to us –

The Iliad, *Oedipus*, *Twelfth Night*,
And 'There's a certain slant of light.'

Poor fools, all mad and middlebrow.
We write so much better now.

LEWIS CARROLL

Poeta Fit, Non Nascitur

'How shall I be a poet?
   How shall I write in rhyme?
You told me once "the very wish
   Partook of the sublime."
Then tell me how! Don't put me off
   With your "another time"!'

The old man smiled to see him,
   To hear his sudden sally;
He liked the lad to speak his mind
   Enthusiastically;
And thought 'There's no hum-drum in him,
   Nor any shilly-shally.'

'And would you be a poet
   Before you've been to school?
Ah, well! I hardly thought you
   So absolute a fool.
First learn to be spasmodic –
   A very simple rule.

'For first you write a sentence,
   And then you chop it small;
Then mix the bits, and sort them out
   Just as they chance to fall:
The order of the phrases makes
   No difference at all.

'Then, if you'd be impressive,
    Remember what I say,
That abstract qualities begin
    With capitals alway:
The True, the Good, the Beautiful –
    Those are the things that pay!

'Next, when you are describing
    A shape, or sound, or tint;
Don't state the matter plainly,
    But put it in a hint;
And learn to look at all things
    With a sort of mental squint.'

'For instance, if I wished, Sir,
    Of mutton-pies to tell,
Should I say "dreams of fleecy flocks
    Pent in a wheaten cell"?'
'Why, yes,' the old man said: 'that phrase
    Would answer very well.'

'Then fourthly, there are epithets
    That suit with any word –
As well as Harvey's Reading Sauce
    With fish or flesh, or bird –
Of these "wild", "lonely", "weary", "strange",
    Are much to be preferred.'

'And will it do, O will it do
    To take them in a lump –
As "the wild man went his weary way
    To a strange and lonely pump"?'
'Nay, nay! You must not hastily
    To such conclusions jump.

'Such epithets, like pepper,
    Give zest to what you write;
And, if you strew them sparely,
    They whet the appetite:
But if you lay them on too thick,
    You spoil the matter quite!

'Last, as to the arrangement:
    Your reader, you should show him,
Must take what information he
    Can get, and look for no im-
Mature disclosure of the drift
    And purpose of your poem.

'Therefore, to test his patience –
    How much he can endure –
Mention no places, names, or dates,
    And evermore be sure
Throughout the poem to be found
    Consistently obscure.

'First fix upon the limit
    To which it shall extend:
Then fill it up with "Padding"
    (Beg some of any friend):
Your great SENSATION-STANZA
    You place towards the end.'

'And what is a Sensation,
    Grandfather, tell me, pray?
I think I never heard the word
    So used before today:
Be kind enough to mention one
    "Exempli gratia" '.

And the old man, looking sadly
   Across the garden lawn,
Where here and there a dew-drop
   Yet glittered in the dawn,
Said "Go to the Adelphi,
   And see the "Colleen Bawn".

'The word is due to Boucicault –
   The theory is his,
Where Life becomes a Spasm,
   And History a Whiz:
If that is not Sensation,
   I don't know what it is.

'Now try your hand, ere Fancy
   Have lost its present glow –'
'And then,' his grandson added,
   'We'll publish it, you know:
Green cloth – gold-lettered at the back –
   In duodecimo!'

Then proudly smiled that old man
   To see the eager lad
Rush madly for his pen and ink
   And for his blotting-pad –
But, when he thought of *publishing*,
   His face grew stern and sad.

To the Author of a Sonnet

beginning ' "Sad is my verse," you say, "and yet no tear" '

Thy verse is 'sad' enough, no doubt:
    A devilish deal more sad than witty!
Why we should weep I can't find out,
    Unless for *thee* we weep in pity.

Yet there is one I pity more;
    And much, alas! I think he needs it;
For he, I'm sure, will suffer sore,
    Who, to his own misfortune, reads it.

Thy rhymes, without the aid of magic,
    May *once* be read – but never after:
Yet their effect's by no means tragic,
    Although by far too dull for laughter.

But would you make our bosoms bleed,
    And of no common pang complain –
If you would make us weep indeed,
    Tell us, you'll read them o'er again.

Ancient Music

Winter is icummen in,
Lhude sing Goddamm,
Raineth drop and staineth slop,
And how the wind doth ramm!
    Sing: Goddamm.
Skiddeth bus and sloppeth us,
An ague hath my ham.
Freezeth river, turneth liver,
    Damn you, sing: Goddamm.
Goddamm, Goddamm, 'tis why I am, Goddamm.
    So 'gainst the winter's balm.
Sing goddamm, damm, sing Goddamm,
Sing goddamm, sing goddamm, DAMM.

R. J. YEATMAN and W. C. SELLAR

How I Brought the Good News from Aix to Ghent
(or Vice Versa)

I sprang to the rollocks and Jorrocks and me,
And I galloped, you galloped, he galloped, we galloped all
   three . . .
Not a word to each other; we kept changing place,
Neck to neck, back to front, ear to ear, face to face;
And we yelled once or twice, when we heard a clock chime,
'Would you kindly oblige us, *Is that the right time?*'
As I galloped, you galloped, he galloped, we galloped, ye
   galloped, they two shall have galloped; *let us trot.*

I unsaddled the saddle, unbuckled the bit,
Unshackled the bridle (the thing didn't fit)
And ungalloped, ungalloped, ungalloped, ungalloped a bit.
Then I cast off my bluff-coat, let my bowler hat fall,
Took off both my boots and my trousers and all –
Drank off my stirrup-cup, felt a bit tight,
And unbridled the saddle: it still wasn't right.

Then all I remember is, things reeling round
As I sat with my head 'twixt my ears on the ground –
For imagine my shame when I asked what I meant
And I had to confess that I'd been, gone and went
And *forgotten the news* I was bringing to Ghent,
Though I'd galloped and galloped and galloped and
   galloped and galloped
And galloped and galloped and galloped. (Had I not would
   have been galloped?)

ENVOI

So I sprang to a taxi and shouted 'To Aix!'
And he blew on his horn and he threw off his brakes,
And all the way back till my money was spent
We rattled and rattled and rattled and rattled and rattled
And rattled and rattled –
And eventually sent a telegram.

The Bards

My aged friend, Miss Wilkinson,
   Whose mother was a Lambe,
Saw Wordsworth once, and Coleridge, too,
   One morning in her 'pram'.[1]

Birdlike the bards stooped over her
   Like fledgling in a nest;
And Wordsworth said, 'Thou harmless babe!'
   And Coleridge was impressed.

The pretty thing gazed up and smiled,
   And softly murmured, 'Coo!'
William was then aged sixty-four
   And Samuel sixty-two.

    1. This was a three wheeled vehicle
      Of iron and of wood;
     It had a leather apron,
       But it hadn't any hood.

Changed

I know not why my soul is rack'd:
  Why I ne'er smile as was my wont:
I only know that, as a fact,
    I don't.
I used to roam o'er glen and glade
  Buoyant and blithe as other folk:
And not unfrequently I made
    A joke.

A minstrel's fire within me burn'd.
  I'd sing, as one whose heart must break,
Lay upon lay: I nearly learn'd
    To shake.
All day I sang; of love, of fame,
  Of fights our fathers fought of yore,
Until the thing almost became
    A bore.

I cannot sing the old songs now!
  It is not that I deem them low;
'Tis that I can't remember how
    They go.
I could not range the hills till high
  Above me stood the summer moon:
And as to dancing, I could fly
    As soon.

The sports, to which with boyish glee
    I sprang erewhile, attract no more;
Although I am but sixty-three
        Or four.
Nay, worse than that, I've seem'd of late
    To shrink from happy boyhood – boys
Have grown so noisy, and I hate
        A noise.

They fright me, when the beech is green,
    By swarming up its stem for eggs:
They drive their horrid hoops between
        My legs: –
It's idle to repine, I know;
    I'll tell you what I'll do instead:
I'll drink my arrowroot, and go
        To bed.

Peekaboo, I Almost See You

Middle-aged life is merry, and I love to lead it,

But there comes a day when your eyes are all right but
    your arm isn't long enough to hold the telephone book
    where you can read it,

And your friends get jocular, so you go to the oculist,

And of all your friends he is the joculist,

So over his facetiousness let us skim,

Only noting that he has been waiting for you ever since
    you said Good evening to his grandfather clock under
    the impression that it was him,

And you look at his chart and it says SHRDLU QWERTYOP,
    and you say Well, why SHRDNTLU QWERTYOP? and he
    says one set of glasses won't do.

You need two,

One for reading Erle Stanley Gardner's Perry Mason and
    Keats's 'Endymion' with,

And the other for walking around without saying Hello to
    strange wymion with.

So you spend your time taking off your seeing glasses to
    put on your reading glasses, and then remembering that
    your reading glasses are upstairs or in the car,

And then you can't find your seeing glasses again because
    without them on you can't see where they are.

Enough of such mishaps, they would try the patience of
    an ox,

I prefer to forget both pairs of glasses and pass my declining
    years saluting strange women and grandfather clocks.

Scintillate

I have outlived
my youthfulness
so a quiet life for me

where once
I used to
scintillate

now I sin
till ten
past three.

J. B. NAYLOR

King David and King Solomon

King David and King Solomon
   Led merry, merry lives,
With many, many lady friends
   And many, many wives;
But when old age crept over them,
   With many, many qualms,
King Solomon wrote the Proverbs,
   And King David wrote the Psalms.

Margin Prayer from an Ancient Psalter

Lord I know, and I know you know I know
this is a drudge's penance. Only dull scholars
or cowherds maddened with cow-watching
will ever read *The Grey Psalter of Antrim*.
I have copied it these thirteen years
waiting for the good bits – High King of the Roads,
are there any good bits in *The Grey Psalter of Antrim*?

(Text illegible here because of teeth-marks.)

It has the magic realism of an argumentum:
it has the narrative subtlety of the Calendar of Oengus;
it has the oblique wit of the Battle-Cathach of the O'Donnells;
it grips like the colophon to The Book of Durrow;
it deconstructs like a canon-table;
it makes St Jerome's Defence of his Vulgate look racy.
I would make a gift of it to Halfdane the Sacker
that he might use it to wipe his wide Danish arse.
Better its volumes intincted our cattle-trough
and cured poor Luke, my three-legged calf,
than sour my wit and spoil my calligraphy.
Luke! White Luke! Truer beast than Ciarán's Dun Cow!
You would rattle the abbot with your soft off-beats
butting his churns and licking salt from his armpits.
Luke, they flayed you, pumiced your skin to a wafer –
such a hide as King Tadhg might die under –
for pages I colour with ox-gall yellow . . .

(Text illegible here because of tear-stains.)

Oh Forgiving Christ of scribes and sinners
intercede for me with the jobbing abbot!
Get me re-assigned to something pagan
with sex and perhaps gratuitous violence
which I might deplore with insular majuscule
and illustrate with Mozarabic complexity
Ad maioram gloriam Dei et Hiberniae,
and lest you think I judge the book too harshly
from pride or a precious sensibility
I have arranged for a second opinion.
Tomorrow our surveyor, Ronan the Barbarian,
will read out loud as only he can read out loud
selected passages from this which I have scored
while marking out his new church in Killaney
in earshot of that well-versed man, King Suibhne . . .

(Text completely illegible from this point
because of lake-water damage and otter dung.)

Desk Duty

My desk has brought me
all my worst fears on a big tray
and left it across my lap.
I'm not allowed to move until I have
eaten everything up.
I push things around on my plate.
I kick the heating pipes.

A piece of worn carpet on the floor
proves how long I've been sitting here
shuffling my feet,
opening and closing drawers,
looking for something I've lost
under piles of official papers and threats,
roofing grants and housing benefits.

Am I married or single?
Employed or self-employed?
What sort of work do I do?
Is my house being used for business
or entertainment purposes? (See Note 3)
If I am resident at my place of work,
who supplies the furniture?

I have cause to suspect myself
of deliberately wasting time
writing my name and place of birth
under 'Who else lives with you?'
It has taken me all day

to find something true to write
under 'Personal Allowances' – or not untrue.

I know all about my little game
of declaring more than I earn
to the Inland Revenue – or was it less?
I'm guilty as hell,
or I wouldn't be sitting here like this
playing footy-footy with my desk.
I'd be upstairs in bed with my bed.

Mr and Mrs R and the Christmas Card List

Shall I cross them off?
It's twenty years since we last met.

Of course Mr R and I once thought
we were made for each other –

Ah, that heart-stopping moment
by the kitchen sink, when he took off

his spectacles and fiercely kissed me.
But all that lasted less than a week

and what I recall more vividly
is Mrs R's good advice:

*Always plunge your lemons in hot water
before you squeeze them.*

One more year perhaps.

On the Circuit

Among Pelagian travellers,
Lost on their lewd conceited way
To Massachusetts, Michigan,
Miami or L.A.,

An airborne instrument I sit,
Predestined nightly to fulfil
Columbia-Giesen-Management's
Unfathomable will,

By whose election justified,
I bring my gospel of the Muse
To fundamentalists, to nuns,
To Gentiles and to Jews,

And daily, seven days a week,
Before a local sense has jelled,
From talking-site to talking-site
Am jet-or-prop-propelled.

Though warm my welcome everywhere
I shift so frequently, so fast,
I cannot now say where I was
The evening before last,

Unless some singular event
Should intervene to save the place,
A truly asinine remark,
A soul-bewitching face,

Or blessed encounter, full of joy,
Unscheduled on the Giesen Plan,
With, here, an addict of Tolkien,
There, a Charles Williams fan.

Since Merit but a dunghill is,
I mount the rostrum unafraid:
Indeed, 'twere damnable to ask
If I am overpaid.

Spirit is willing to repeat
Without a qualm the same old talk,
But Flesh is homesick for our snug
Apartment in New York.

A sulky fifty-six, he finds
A change of mealtime utter hell,
Grown far too crotchety to like
A luxury hotel.

The Bible is a goodly book
I always can peruse with zest,
But really cannot say the same
For Hilton's *Be My Guest*,

Nor bear with equanimity
The radio in students' cars,
Musak at breakfast, or – dear God! –
Girl-organists in bars.

Then, worst of all the anxious thought,
Each time my plane begins to sink
And the No Smoking sign comes on:
What will there be to drink?

Is this a milieu where I must
How grahamgreeneish! How infra dig!
Snatch from the bottle in my bag
An analeptic swig?

Another morning comes: I see,
Dwindling below me on the plane,
The roofs of one more audience
I shall not see again.

God bless the lot of them, although
I don't remember which was which:
God bless the U.S.A., so large,
So friendly, and so rich.

Vindaloo in Merthyr Tydfil

The first night of my second voyage to Wales,
tired as rag from ascending the left cheek of Earth,
I nevertheless went to Merthyr in good company
and warm in neckclothing and speech in the Butcher's Arms
till Time struck us pintless, and Eddie Rees steamed in brick
    lanes
and under the dark of the White Tip we repaired shouting

to I think the Bengal. I called for curry, the hottest,
vain of my nation, proud of my hard mouth from childhood,
the kindly brown waiter wringing the hands of dissuasion
O vindaloo, sir! You sure you want vindaloo, sir?
But I cried Yes please, being too far in to go back,
the bright bells of Rhymney moreover sang in my brains.

Fair play, it was frightful. I spooned the chicken of Hell
in a sauce of rich yellow brimstone. The valley boys with me
tasting it, croaked to white Jesus. And only pride drove me,
forkful by forkful, observed by hot mangosteen eyes,
by all the carnivorous castes and gurus from Cardiff
my brilliant tears washing the unbelief of the Welsh.

Oh it was a ride on Watneys plunging red barrel
through all the burning ghats of most carnal ambition
and never again will I want such illumination
for three days on end concerning my own mortal coil
but I signed my plate in the end with a licked knife and fork
and green-and-gold spotted, I sang for my pains like the free
before I passed out among all the stars of Cilfynydd.

Extra Helpings

In our primary school
Set lunch was the rule
Though in Scotland we called that meal 'dinner'.
We tucked in like starvelings,
Inchinnan's wee darlings,
And it didn't make thin children thinner.

But what I liked best
Was disliked by the rest,
Rice pudding with raisins and bloated sultanas,
Stewed fruit and dumplings
In big extra helpings
And hooray for first post-War bananas!
 It was very good scoff
 So I polished it off
  A very dab hand with a spoon,
   a spoon,
  A very dab hand with my spoon.

Detested mashed turnip
Gave most kids the pip
While cabbage was much the same tale.
No shortage of roots, and no hardship of greens –
After mine I ate Harry's, then Elspeth's, then Jean's,
O a glutton for turnips and kail.
 It was very good scoff
 So I polished it off
  A very dab hand with a fork,
   a fork,
  A very dab hand with my fork.

I used to be slim.
I used to be *slim*!
'Look!' they say now. 'There's at least *three* of him!'
To which I reply
With a daggerly eye,
'Well, that's better than three-quarters *you*!'
But my clothes don't fit
I'm fed up with it
And the sylph in me's guilty and blue.

> *Semolina and sago with jam,*
>> *with jam,*
> *Oh dear, what a pudding I am,*
>> *I am,*
> *Oh dear, what a pudding I am.*

But I'm longing for lunch
And something to munch
Though I wish it was back in that school
When the dinner-bell rings
And all good things
Await to be guzzled until I am happy and full.
Dear God, I'd die
For Shepherd's Pie
In 1949 or 1950
When the dinner-bell rings
And all good things
Draw children on the sniff and make them nifty.

> *It was very good scoff*
> *So I polished it off –*
>> *Oh dear, what a pudding I am,*
>>> *I am,*

Oh dear, what a pudding I am,
But a very dab hand with a spoon,
A spoon,
And a very dab hand with a fork.

ANONYMOUS

Through the Teeth

Through the teeth
And past the gums.
Look out stomach,
Here it comes!

Epicurean Reminiscences of a Sentimentalist

'My *Tables! Meat* it is, *I set it* down!' *Hamlet*

I think it was Spring – but not certain I am –
  When my passion began first to work;
But I know we were certainly looking for lamb,
  And the season was over for pork.

'Twas at Christmas, I think, when I met with Miss
    Chase,
  Yes, – for Morris had asked me to dine, –
And I thought I had never beheld such a face,
  Or so noble a turkey and chine.

Placed close to her side, it make others quite wild,
  With sheer envy to witness my luck;
How she blushed as I gave her some turtle, and smiled
  As I afterwards offered some duck.

I looked and I languished, alas, to my cost,
  Through three courses of dishes and meats;
Getting deeper in love – but my heart was quite lost,
  When it came to the trifle and sweets!

With a rent-roll that told of my houses and land
  To her parents I told my designs –
And then to herself I presented my hand,
  With a very fine pottle of pines!*

I asked her to have me for weal or for woe,
  And she did not object in the least:
I can't tell the date – but we married, I know,
  Just in time to have game at the feast.

We went to —, it certainly was the seaside;
  For the next, the most blessed of morns,
I remember how fondly I gazed at my bride,
  Sitting down to a plateful of prawns.

Oh, never may mem'ry lose sight of that year,
  But still hallow the time as it ought,
That season the 'grass'[†] was remarkably dear,
  And the peas at a guinea a quart.

So happy, like hours, all our days seemed to haste,
  A fond pair, such as poets have drawn,
So united in heart – so congenial in taste,
  We were both of us partial to brawn!

A long life I looked for of bliss with my bride,
  But then Death – I ne'er dreamt about that!
Oh, there's nothing certain in life, as I cried,
  When my turbot eloped with the cat!

My dearest took ill at the turn of the year,
  But the cause no physician could nab;
But something it seemed like consumption, I fear,
  It was just after supping on crab.

In vain she was doctored, in vain she was dosed,
  Still her strength and her appetite pined;
She lost relish for what she had relished the most,
  Even salmon she deeply declined.

For months still I lingered in hope and in doubt,
  While her form it grew wasted and thin;
But the last dying spark of existence went out,
  As the oysters were just coming in!

She died, and she left me the saddest of men
   To indulge in a widower's moan;
Oh, I felt all the power of solitude then,
   As I ate my first natives alone!

But when I beheld Virtue's friends in their cloaks,
   And with sorrowful crape on their hats,
Oh, my grief poured a flood! and the out-of-door folks
   Were all crying – I think it was sprats!

           *basket of pineapples   †asparagus

The Virtues of Carnation Milk

(This quatrain is imagined as the caption under a picture of a rugged-looking cowboy seated upon a bale of hay.)

Carnation Milk is the best in the land;
Here I sit with a can in my hand –
No tits to pull, no hay to pitch,
You just punch a hole in the son of a bitch.

How the Wild South East was Lost

For Robert Maclean

See, I was raised on the wild side, border country,
Kent 'n' Surrey, a spit from the county line,
An' they bring me up in a prep school over the canyon:
Weren't no irregular verb I couldn't call mine.

Them days, I seen oldtimers set in the ranch-house
(Talkin' 'bout J. 'Boy' Hobbs and Pat C. Hendren)
Blow a man clean away with a Greek optative,
Scripture test, or a sprig o' that rho-do-dendron.

Hard pedallin' country, stranger, flint 'n' chalkface,
Evergreen needles, acorns an' beechmast shells,
But atop that old lone pine you could squint clean over
To the dome o' the Chamber o' Commerce in Tunbridge
    Wells.

Yep, I was raised in them changeable weather conditions:
I seen 'em, afternoon of a sunny dawn,
Clack up the deck chairs, bolt for the back French windows
When they bin drinkin' that strong tea on the lawn.

In a cloud o' pipesmoke rollin' there over the canyon,
Book-larned me up that Minor Scholarship stuff:
Bent my back to that in-between innings light roller
And life weren't easy. And that's why I'm so tough.

KENNETH GRAHAME

The Song of Mr Toad

The world has held great Heroes,
    As history books have showed;
But never a name to go down to fame
    Compared with that of Toad!

The clever men at Oxford
    Know all that there is to be knowed,
But they none of them knew one half as much
    As intelligent Mr Toad!

The animals sat in the Ark and cried,
    Their tears in torrents flowed.
Who was it said, 'There's land ahead'?
    Encouraging Mr Toad!

The Army all saluted
    As they marched along the road.
Was it the King? Or Kitchener?
    No. It was Mr Toad!

The Queen and her Ladies-in-waiting
    Sat at the window and sewed.
She cried, 'Look! who's that *handsome* man?'
    They answered, 'Mr Toad.'

Very Simply Topping Up the Brake Fluid

Yes, love, that's why the warning light comes on. Don't
panic. Fetch some universal brake-fluid
and a five-eighths screwdriver from your toolkit
then prop the bonnet open. Go on, it won't

eat you. Now, without slicing through the fan-belt
try and slide the sharp end of the screwdriver
under the lid and push the spade connector
through its bed, go on, that's it. Now you're all right

to unscrew, no, clockwise, you see it's Russian
love, back to front, that's it. You see, it's empty.
Now, gently with your hand and I mean gently,
try and create a bit of space by pushing

the float-chamber sideways so there's room to pour,
gently does it, that's it. Try not to spill, it's
corrosive: rusts, you know, and fill it till it's
level with the notch on the clutch reservoir.

Lovely. There's some Swarfega in the office
if you want a wash and some soft roll above
the cistern for, you know. Oh don't mind him, love,
he doesn't bite. Come here and sit down Prince. Prince!

Now, where's that bloody alternator? Managed?
Oh any time, love. I'll not charge you for that
because it's nothing of a job. If you want
us again we're in the book. Tell your husband.

Men Talk

(Rap)

Women
Rabbit rabbit rabbit women
Tattle and titter
Women prattle
Women waffle and witter

Men Talk. Men Talk.

Women into Girl Talk
About Women's Trouble
Trivia 'n' Small Talk
They yap and they babble

Men Talk. Men Talk.

Women yatter
Women chatter
Women chew the fat, women spill the beans
Women aint been takin'
The oh-so Good Advice in them
Women's Magazines.

A Man Likes A Good Listener.

Oh yeah
I like A Woman
Who likes me enough
Not to nitpick
Not to nag and
Not to interrupt 'cause I call that treason
A woman with the Good Grace

To be struck dumb
By me Sweet Reason. Yes –

A Man Likes a Good Listener

A Real
Man
Likes a Real Good Listener

Women yap yap yap
Verbal Diarrhoea is a Female Disease
Woman she spread she rumours round she
Like Philadelphia Cream Cheese.

Oh
Bossy Women Gossip
Girlish Women Giggle
Women natter, women nag
Women niggle niggle niggle

Men Talk.

Men
Think First, Speak Later
Men Talk.

Ode on a Goal
for Andrew Bolton

How good was Gascoigne's goal?
As good as the tarts the knave stole,
As good as a cream-stuffed profiterole
Wolfed whole.

And how good was his left foot?
Better than the one in his right boot
With which he elected to shoot?
That's moot.

Suffice it to say his first touch
Left little but straws at which to clutch.
Too good for the Scots? – Or the Dutch,
Oh, much.

So talk not the haircut,
The incipient beer-gut
Or of the man's being a fruit-and-nut
Case, but

Savour simply the sublime control
Like angels performing rock 'n' roll
On the dance-floor of a pinhead. Extol
That goal!

Etiquette

The *Ballyshannon* foundered off the coast of Cariboo,
And down in fathoms many went the captain and the crew;
Down went the owners – greedy men whom hope of gain
    allured:
Oh, dry the starting tear, for they were heavily insured.

Besides the captain and the mate, the owners and the crew,
The passengers were also drowned excepting only two:
Young Peter Gray, who tasted teas for Baker, Croop and Co.,
And Somers, who from Eastern shores imported indigo.

These passengers, by reason of their clinging to a mast,
Upon a desert island were eventually cast.
They hunted for their meals, as Alexander Selkirk used,
But they couldn't chat together – they had not been
    introduced.

For Peter Gray, and Somers too, though certainly in trade,
Were properly particular about the friends they made;
And somehow thus they settled it without a word of
    mouth –
That Gray should take the northern half, while Somers
    took the south.

On Peter's portion oysters grew – a delicacy rare,
But oysters were a delicacy Peter couldn't bear.
On Somers' side was turtle, on the shingle lying thick,
Which Somers couldn't eat, because it always made him
    sick.

Gray gnashed his teeth with envy as he saw a mighty store
Of turtle unmolested on his fellow-creature's shore:
The oysters at his feet aside impatiently he shoved,
For turtle and his mother were the only things he loved.

And Somers sighed in sorrow as he settled in the south,
For the thought of Peter's oysters brought the water to his
    mouth.
He longed to lay him down upon the shelly bed, and stuff:
He had often eaten oysters, but had never had enough.

How they wished an introduction to each other they had
    had
When on board the *Ballyshannon!* And it drove them
    nearly mad
To think how very friendly with each other they might get,
If it wasn't for the arbitrary rule of etiquette!

One day, when out a-hunting for the *mus ridiculus*,
Gray overheard his fellow-man soliloquising thus:
'I wonder how the playmates of my youth are getting on,
McConnell, S. B. Walters, Paddy Byles, and Robinson?'

These simple words made Peter as delighted as could be,
Old chummies at the Charterhouse were Robinson and he!
He walked straight up to Somers, then he turned extremely
    red,
Hesitated, hummed and hawed a bit, then cleared his
    throat, and said:

'I beg your pardon – pray forgive me if I seem too bold,
But you have breathed a name I knew familiarly of old.
You spoke aloud of Robinson – I happened to be by –
You know him?' 'Yes, extremely well.' 'Allow me – so do I!'

It was enough: they felt they could more sociably get on,
For (ah, the magic of the fact!) they each knew Robinson!
And Mr Somers' turtle was at Peter's service quite,
And Mr Somers punished Peter's oyster-beds all night.

They soon became like brothers from community of
    wrongs:
They wrote each other little odes and sang each other
    songs;
They told each other anecdotes disparaging their wives;
On several occasions, too, they saved each other's lives.

They felt quite melancholy when they parted for the night,
And got up in the morning soon as ever it was light;
Each other's pleasant company they reckoned so upon,
And all because it happened that they both knew
    Robinson!

They lived for many years on that inhospitable shore,
And day by day they learned to love each other more and
    more.
At last, to their astonishment, on getting up one day,
They saw a vessel anchored in the offing of the bay!

To Peter an idea occurred. 'Suppose we cross the main?
So good an opportunity may not occur again.'
And Somers thought a minute, then ejaculated, 'Done!
I wonder how my business in the City's getting on?'

'But stay,' said Mr Peter: 'when in England, as you know,
I earned a living tasting teas for Baker, Croop and Co.,
I may be superseded – my employers think me dead!'
'Then come with me,' said Somers, 'and taste indigo
    instead.'

But all their plans were scattered in a moment when they
    found
The vessel was a convict ship from Portland, outward
    bound!
When a boat came off to fetch them, though they felt it very
    kind,
To go on board they firmly but respectfully declined.

As both the happy settlers roared with laughter at the joke,
They recognised an unattractive fellow pulling stroke:
'Twas Robinson – a convict, in an unbecoming frock!
Condemned to seven years for misappropriating stock!!!

They laughed no more, for Somers thought he had been
    rather rash
In knowing one whose friend had misappropriated cash;
And Peter thought a foolish tack he must have gone upon
In making the acquaintance of a friend of Robinson.

At first they didn't quarrel very openly, I've heard;
They nodded when they met, and now and then exchanged
    a word:
The word grew rare, and rarer still the nodding of the head,
And when they meet each other now, they cut each other
    dead.

To allocate the island they agreed by word of mouth,
And Peter takes the north again, and Somers takes the
    south;
And Peter has the oysters, which he loathes with horror
    grim,
And Somers has the turtle – turtle disagrees with him.

D. J. ENRIGHT

from Paradise Illustrated: A Sequence

I

'Come!' spoke the Almighty to Adam.
'There's work to do, even in Eden.'

'I want to see what you'll call them,'
The Lord said. 'It's a good day for it.'
'And take your thumb out of your mouth,'
He added. (Adam was missing his mother.)

So they shuffled past, or they hopped,
Or they waddled. The beasts of the field
And the fowls of the air,
Pretending not to notice him.

'Speak up now,' said the Lord God briskly.
'Give each and every one the name thereof.'

'Fido,' said Adam, thinking hard,
As the animals went past him one by one,
'Bambi', 'Harpy', 'Pooh',
'Incitatus', 'Acidosis', 'Apparat',
'Krafft-Ebing', 'Indo-China', 'Schnorkel',
'Buggins', 'Bollock' –

'Bullock will do,' said the Lord God, 'I like it.
The rest are rubbish. You must try again tomorrow.'

'Can't you let *her* name something?'
Begged Adam. 'She's always on at me
About the animals.'

'Herself a fairer flower,'
Murmured God. 'Hardly necessary,
I would say. But if it makes her happy . . .'

*

'What a trek!' Eve muttered.
'The animals *came* to Adam . . .
Well, Mohammed must go to the mountain.'

'What's that you said?' the Almighty asked.
But she was on her way.

*

'Lady's finger,' said Eve.
'Lady's smock.
Lady's slipper.
Lady's tresses . . .'

She paused.
'Adam's apple.'

'No,' said the Lord,
'Strike that out.'

'Old man's beard, then.'
She sped towards the mountain.

'Lily.
Rose.
Violet.
Daisy.
Poppy.
Amaryllis.
Eglantine.
Veronica.
Marigold.
Iris.
Marguerite.
Pansy.
Petunia.
Jasmine.
May.'

'I'm worn out,' she gasped.
'Belladonna –
And that's all for today.'

*

'She's better at names than you were,'
The Lord observed.
'They all sound womanish to me,'
Said Adam, nettled.

XXII

'Why didn't we think of clothes before?'
Asked Adam,
Removing Eve's.

'Why did we ever think of clothes?'
Asked Eve,
Laundering Adam's.

JOHN AGARD

On First-Name Terms

Hey. None of this Beelzebub business.
Lighten up. No more Prince of Darkness
and all that Devil's Advocate
kind of stuff. I'm your mate.
It's all right to call me Dev
and I'll call you Les or Mags or Trev.
Formality stinks. Don't say evil. Say Ev.

No Peas for the Wicked

No peas for the wicked
No carrots for the damned
No parsnips for the naughty
    O Lord we pray

No sprouts for the shameless
No cabbage for the shady
No lettuce for the lecherous
    No way, no way

No potatoes for the deviants
No radish for the riff-raff
No spinach for the spineless
    Lock them away

No beetroot for the boasters
No mange-tout for the mobsters
No corn-on-the-cob et cetera
    (Shall we call it a day?)

Deep Sorriness Atonement Song

(for missed appointment, BBC North, Manchester)

The man who sold Manhattan for a halfway decent bangle,
He had talks with Adolf Hitler and could see it from his
    angle,
And he heard the Silver Beatles but he didn't think they'd
    make it
So he chose a cake on Pudding Lane and thought 'Oh well
    I'll bake it',
        But his chances they were slim,
        And his brothers they were Grimm,
        And he's sorry, very sorry,
        But I'm sorrier than him.

And the drunken plastic surgeon who said 'I know, let's
    enlarge 'em!'
And the bloke who told the Light Brigade 'Oh what the
    hell, let's charge 'em,'
The magician with an early evening gig on the *Titanic*,
And the Mayor who told the people of Atlantis not to panic,
        And the Dong about his nose,
        And the Pobble *re* his toes,
        They're all sorry, very sorry,
        But I'm sorrier than those.

And don't forget the Bible, with the Sodomites and Judas,
And Onan who discovered something nothing was as rude
    as,
And anyone who reckoned it was City's year for Wembley,
And the kid who called Napoleon a shortarse in assembly,
        And the man who always smiles

'Cause he knows I have his files,
They're all sorry, really sorry,
But I'm sorrier by miles.

And Robert Falcon Scott who lost the race to a Norwegian,
And anyone who's ever spilt the pint of a Glaswegian,
Or told a Finn a joke or spent an hour with a Swiss-
    German,
Or got a mermaid in the sack and found it was a merman,
        Or him who smelt a rat,
        And got curious as a cat,
        They're all sorry, deeply sorry,
        But I'm sorrier than that.

All the people who were rubbish when we needed them to
    do it,
Whose wires crossed, whose spirit failed, who ballsed it up
    or blew it,
All notchers of *nul points* and all who have a problem
    Houston,
At least they weren't in Kensington when they should
    have been at Euston.
        For I didn't build the Wall
        And I didn't cause the Fall
        But I'm sorry, Lord I'm sorry,
        I'm the sorriest of all.

Things

There are worse things than having behaved foolishly in
   public.
There are worse things than these miniature betrayals,
committed or endured or suspected; there are worse things
than not being able to sleep for thinking about them.
It is 5 a.m. All the worse things come stalking in
and stand icily about the bed looking worse and worse and
   worse.

The Skip

I took my life and threw it on the skip,
Reckoning the next-door neighbours wouldn't mind
If my life hitched a lift to the council tip
With their dry rot and rubble. What you find

With skips is – the whole community joins in.
Old mattresses appear, doors kind of drift
Along with all that won't fit in the bin
And what the bin-men can't be fished to shift.

I threw away my life, and there it lay
And grew quite sodden. 'What a dreadful shame,'
Clucked some old bag and sucked her teeth: 'The way
The young these days . . . no values . . . me, I blame . . .'

But I blamed no one. Quality control
Had loused it up, and that was that. 'Nough said.
I couldn't stick at home. I took a stroll
And passed the skip, and left my life for dead.

Without my life, the beer was just as foul,
The landlord still as filthy as his wife,
The chicken in the basket was an owl,
And no one said: 'Ee, Jim-lad, whur's thee life?'

Well, I got back that night the worse for wear,
But still just capable of single vision;
Looked in the skip; my life – it wasn't there!
Some bugger'd nicked it – *without* my permission.

Okay, so I got angry and began
To shout, and woke the street. Okay. *Okay!*
And I was sick all down the neighbour's van.
And I disgraced myself on the par-*kay*.

And then . . . you know how if you've had a few
You'll wake at dawn, all healthy, like sea breezes,
Raring to go, and thinking: 'Clever you!
You've got away with it.' And then, oh Jesus,

It hits you. Well, that morning, just at six
I woke, got up and looked down at the skip.
There lay my life, still sodden, on the bricks;
There lay my poor old life, arse over tip.

Or was it mine? Still dressed, I went downstairs
And took a long cool look. The truth was dawning.
Someone had just exchanged my life for theirs.
Poor fool, I thought – I should have left a warning.

Some bastard saw my life and thought it nicer
Than what he had. Yet what he'd had seemed fine.
He'd never caught his fingers in the slicer
The way I'd managed in that life of mine.

His life lay glistening in the rain, neglected,
Yet still a decent, an authentic life.
Some people I can think of, I reflected
Would take that thing as soon as you'd say Knife.

It seemed a shame to miss a chance like that.
I brought the life in, dried it by the stove.
It looked so fetching, stretched out on the mat.
I tried it on. It fitted, like a glove.

And now, when some local bat drops off the twig
And new folk take the house, and pull up floors
And knock down walls and hire some kind of big
Container (say, a skip) for their old doors,

I'll watch it like a hawk, and every day
I'll make at least – oh – half a dozen trips.
I've furnished an existence in that way.
You'd not believe the things you find on skips.

OGDEN NASH

Family Court

One would be in less danger
From the wiles of the stranger
If one's own kin and kith
Were more fun to be with.

Discipline

To Percival, my youngest son,
Who cut his sister's throat, for fun,
I said: 'Now, Percy! Manners, please!
You really mustn't be a tease!
I shall refuse, another time,
To take you to the Pantomime!'

A Parental Ode to My Son, Aged Three Years and Four Months

Thou happy, happy elf!
(But stop – first let me kiss away that tear),
    Thou tiny image of myself!
(My love, he's poking peas into his ear)
    Thou merry laughing sprite!
    With spirits feather-light,
Untouched by sorrow and unsoiled by sin –
(Good heavens! the child is swallowing a pin!)

    Thou tricksy Puck!
With antic toys so funnily bestuck,
Light as the singing bird that wings the air
(The door! the door! he'll tumble down the stair!)
    Thou darling of thy sire!
(Why, Jane, he'll set his pinafore on fire)
    Thou imp of mirth and joy,
In Love's dear chain so strong and bright a link,
Thou idol of thy parents – (drat the boy!
    There goes my ink!)

    Thou cherub! – but of earth,
Fit playfellow for Fays by moonlight pale,
    In harmless sport and mirth,
(That dog will bite him if he pulls its tail)
    Thou human honey-bee, extracting honey
From every blossom in the world that blows,
    Singing in youth's Elysium ever sunny –
(Another tumble! – that's his precious nose!)

Thy father's pride and hope
(He'll break the mirror with that skipping-rope!)
With pure heart newly stamped from Nature's mint
(Where *did* he learn that squint?)
    Thou young domestic dove!
(He'll have that jug off with another shove!)
  Dear nursling of the hymeneal nest!
  (Are those torn clothes his best!)
    Little epitome of man!
(He'll climb upon the table, that's his plan!)
Touched with the beauteous trials of dawning life –
    (He's got a knife!)

    Thou enviable being!
No storms, no clouds, in thy blue sky foreseeing,
    Play on, play on,
    My elfin John!
Toss the light ball – bestride the stick,
(I knew so many cakes would make him sick!)
With fancies buoyant as the thistledown,
Prompting the face grotesque, and antic brisk,
    With many a lamblike frisk –
(He's got the scissors, snipping at your gown!)

    Thou pretty opening rose!
(Go to your mother, child, and wipe your nose!)
Balmy and breathing music like the south,
(He really brings my heart into my mouth!)
Fresh as the morn, and brilliant as its star,
(I wish that window had an iron bar!)
Bold as the hawk, yet gentle as the dove –
    (I'll tell you what, my love,
I cannot write unless he's sent above.)

STANLEY J. SHARPLESS

Hamlet

Prince Hamlet thought Uncle a traitor
For having it off with his Mater;
    Revenge Dad or not?
    That's the gist of the plot,
And he did – nine soliloquies later.

Ballade of Suicide

The gallows in my garden, people say,
Is new and neat and adequately tall.
I tie the noose on in a knowing way
As one that knots his necktie for a ball;
But just as all the neighbours – on the wall –
Are drawing a long breath to shout 'Hurray!'
The strangest whim has seized me . . . After all
I think I will not hang myself today.

Tomorrow is the time I get my pay –
My uncle's sword is hanging in the hall –
I see a little cloud all pink and grey –
Perhaps the rector's mother will not call –
I fancy that I heard from Mr Gall
That mushrooms could be cooked another way –
I never read the works of Juvenal –
I think I will not hang myself today.

The world will have another washing day;
The decadents decay; the pedants pall;
And H. G. Wells has found that children play,
And Bernard Shaw discovered that they squall;
Rationalists are growing rational –
And through thick woods one finds a stream astray,
So secret that the very sky seems small –
I think I will not hang myself today.

ENVOI

Prince, I can hear the trump of Germinal,
The tumbrils toiling up the terrible way;
Even today your royal head may fall –
I think I will not hang myself today.

The Orbison Consolations

Only the lonely
Know the way you feel tonight?
Surely the poorly
Have *some* insight?
Oddly, the godly
Also might,
And slowly the lowly
Will learn to read you right.

Simply the pimply
Have some idea.
Quaintly the saintly
Have got quite near.
Quickly the sickly
Empathise
And prob'ly the knobbly
Look deep into your eyes.

Rumly, the comely
Will understand.
Shortly the portly
Will take your hand.
Early the surly
Dispraised and panned,
But lately the stately
Have joined your saraband.

Only the lonely
Know the way you feel tonight?
Singly the tingly
Conceive your plight,
But *doubly* the bubbly
Fly your kite . . .

And lastly the ghastly
Know the way you feel tonight.

DOROTHY PARKER

Résumé

Razors pain you;
Rivers are damp;
Acids stain you;
And drugs cause cramp.
Guns aren't lawful;
Nooses give;
Gas smells awful;
You might as well live.

The Pessimist

Nothing to do but work,
    Nothing to eat but food,
Nothing to wear but clothes,
    To keep one from going nude.

Nothing to breathe but air,
    Quick as a flash 'tis gone;
Nowhere to fall but off,
    Nowhere to stand but on.

Nothing to comb but hair,
    Nowhere to sleep but in bed,
Nothing to weep but tears,
    Nothing to bury but dead.

Nothing to sing but songs,
    Ah, well, alas! alack!
Nowhere to go but out,
    Nowhere to come but back.

Nothing to see but sights,
    Nothing to quench but thirst.
Nothing to have but what we've got.
    Thus thro' life we are cursed.

The Dead Alive

When a bore gets hold of me,
  Dull and overbearing,
Be so kind as pray for me,
  I'm as dead as herring.
When the thrusts of Pleasure glib
  In my sides are sticking,
Poking fun at every rib,
  I'm alive and kicking.

When a snob his £ s. d.
  Jingles in his breeches,
Be so kind as pray for me,
  I'm as dead as ditches.
When a birthday's champagne-corks
  Round my ears are clicking,
Marking time with well-oil'd works,
  I'm alive and kicking.

Kings and their supremacy
  Occupy the table,
Be so kind as pray for me,
  I'm as dead as Abel.
Talk about the age of wine
  (Bought by cash or ticking),
So you bring a sample fine,
  I'm alive and kicking.

When a trip to Muscovy
   Tempts a conquest glutton,
Be so kind as pray for me,
   I'm as dead as mutton.
Match me with a tippling foe,
   See who first wants picking
From the dead man's field below
   I'm alive and kicking.

When great scribes to poetry
   March, by notions big led,
Be so kind as pray for me,
   I'm as dead as pig-lead.
When you start a careless song,
   Not at grammar sticking,
Good to push the wine along,
   I'm alive and kicking.

Translated from the French
by Robert B. Brough

The Mummy

(*The mummy* [of Rameses II] *was met at Orly airport by*
Mme Saunier-Seïté. – News item, Sept. 1976)

– May I welcome Your Majesty to Paris.

– Mm.

– I hope the flight from Cairo was reasonable.

– Mmmmm.

– We have a germ-proof room at the Museum of Man
  where we trust Your Majesty will have peace and quiet.

– Unh – unh.

– I am sorry, but this is necessary.
  Your Majesty's person harbours a fungus.

– Fng fng's, hn?

– Well, it is something attacking your cells.
  Your Majesty is gently deteriorating
  after nearly four thousand years
  becalmed in masterly embalmment.
  We wish to save you from the worm.

– Wrm hrm! Mgh-mgh-mgh.

– Indeed I know it must be distressing
  to a pharaoh and a son of Ra,
  to the excavator of Abu Simbel
  that glorious temple in the rock,
  to the perfecter of Karnak hall,
  to the hammer of the Hittites,

[107]

to the colossus whose colossus
raised in red granite at holy Thebes
sixteen-men-high astounds the desert
shattered, as Your Majesty in life
shattered the kingdom and oppressed the poor
with such lavish grandeur and panache,
to Rameses, to Ozymandias,
to the Louis Quatorze of the Nile,
how bitter it must be to feel
a microbe eat your camphored bands.
But we are here to help your Majesty.
We shall encourage you to unwind.
You have many useful years ahead.

– M' n'm 'z 'zym'ndias, kng'v kngz!

– Yes yes. Well, Shelley is dead now.
He was not embalmed. He will not write
about Your Majesty again.

– T't'nkh'm'n? H'tsh'ps't?
'khn't'n? N'f'rt'ti? Mm? Mm?

– The hall of fame has many mansions.
Your Majesty may rest assured
your deeds will always be remembered.

– Youmm w'm'nn. B't'flll w'm'nnnn.
No w'm'nn f'r th'znd' y'rz.

– Your Majesty, what are you doing?

– Ng! Mm. Mhm. Mm? Mm? Mmmmm.

– Your Majesty, Your Majesty! You'll break your stitches!

– Fng st'chez fng's wrm hrm.

– I really hate to have to use
  a hypodermic on a mummy,
  but we cannot have you strain yourself.
  Remember your fungus, Your Majesty.

– Fng. Zzzzzzzz.

– That's right.

– Aaaaaaaaah.

Doubt

I sometimes think I'd rather crow
And be a rooster than to roost
And be a crow. But I dunno.

A rooster he can roost also,
Which don't seem fair when crows can't crow.
Which may help, some. Still I dunno.

Crows should be glad of one thing, though;
Nobody thinks of eating crow,
While roosters they are good enough
For anyone unless they're tough.

There are lots of tough old roosters though,
And anyway a crow can't crow,
So mebby roosters stand more show.
It looks that way. But I dunno.

The Frog

What a wonderful bird the frog are –
When he stand he sit almost;
When he hop, he fly almost.
He ain't got no sense hardly;
He ain't got no tail hardly either.
When he sit, he sit on what he ain't got almost.

O Have You Caught the Tiger?

O have you caught the tiger?
   And can you hold him tight?
And what immortal hand or eye
Could frame his fearful symmetry?
   And does he try to bite?

Yes, I have caught the tiger,
   And he was hard to catch.
O tiger, tiger, do not try
To put your tail into my eye,
   And do not bite and scratch.

Yes, I have caught the tiger.
   O tiger, do not bray!
And what immortal hand or eye
Could frame his fearful symmetry
   I should not like to say.

And may I see the tiger?
   I should indeed delight
To see so large an animal
Without a voyage to Bengal.
   And mind you hold him tight.

Yes, you may see the tiger;
   It will amuse you much.
The tiger is, as you will find,
A creature of the feline kind.
   And mind you do not touch.

And do you feed the tiger,
    And do you keep him clean?
He has a less contented look
Than in the Natural History book,
    And seems a trifle lean.

Oh yes, I feed the tiger,
    And soon he will be plump;
I give him groundsel fresh and sweet,
And much canary-seed to eat,
    And wash him at the pump.

It seems to me the tiger
    Has not been lately fed,
Not for a day or two at least;
And that is why the noble beast
    Has bitten off your head.

Rat, O Rat . . .

never in all my life have I seen
as handsome a rat as you.
Thank you for noticing my potatoes.

O Rat, I am not rich.
I left you a note concerning my potatoes,
but I see that I placed it too high
and you could not read it.

O Rat, my wife and I are cursed
with the possession of a large and hungry dog;
it worries us that he might learn your name –
which is forever on our lips.

O Rat, consider my neighbour:
he has eight children (all of them older
and more intelligent than mine)
and if you lived in his house, Rat,

ten good Christians
(if we include his wife)
would sing your praises nightly,
whereas in my house there are only five.

The British Journalist

You cannot hope
    to bribe or twist,
thank God! the
    British journalist.

But, seeing what
    the man will do
unbribed, there's
    no occasion to.

Publishers

They fuck you up, do publishers.
Against them there is no defence.
No letter, postcard, phone-call stirs
The puddle of their indolence.

Each author's fucked up in his turn.
Each contract is a poison pellet.
And specially must poets learn
That verse don't sell, and they don't sell it.

Man hands on manuscript to man,
Who leaves the thing in St Tropez.
Get out as quickly as you can
And write a television play.

To an American Publisher

You say I must write *another* book? But I've just written
    this one.
You liked it so much that's the reason? Read it again then.

I Had a Duck-Billed Platypus

I had a duck-billed platypus when I was up at Trinity,
With whom I soon discovered a remarkable affinity.
He used to live in lodgings with myself and Arthur Purvis,
And we all went up together for the Diplomatic Service.
I had a certain confidence, I own, in his ability,
He mastered all the subjects with remarkable facility;
And Purvis, though more dubious, agreed that he was
    clever,
But no one else imagined he had any chance whatever.
I failed to pass the interview, the Board with wry grimaces
Took exception to my boots and then objected to my braces,
And Purvis too was failed by an intolerant examiner
Who said he had his doubts as to his sock-suspenders'
    stamina.
The bitterness of failure was considerably mollified,
However, by the ease with which our platypus had
    qualified.
The wisdom of the choice, it soon appeared, was undeniable;
There never was a diplomat more thoroughly reliable.
He never made rash statements his enemies might hold
    him to,
He never stated anything, for no one ever told him to,
And soon he was appointed, so correct was his behaviour,
Our Minister (without Portfolio) to Trans-Moravia.
My friend was loved and honoured from the Andes to
    Esthonia,
He soon achieved a pact between Peru and Patagonia,
He never vexed the Russians nor offended the Rumanians,
He pacified the Letts and yet appeased the Lithuanians,

Won approval from his masters down in Downing Street so
    wholly, O,
He was soon to be rewarded with the grant of a Portfolio.

When, on the Anniversary of Greek Emancipation,
Alas! He laid an egg in the Bulgarian Legation.
This untoward occurrence caused unheard-of
    repercussions,
Giving rise to epidemics of sword-clanking in the Prussians.
The Poles began to threaten, and the Finns began to flap
    at him,
Directing all the blame for this unfortunate mishap at him;
While the Swedes withdrew entirely from the Anglo-Saxon
    dailies
The right of photographing the Aurora Borealis,
And, all efforts at rapprochement in the meantime proving
    barren,
The Japanese in self-defence annexed the Isle of Arran.
My platypus, once thought to be more cautious and more
    tentative
Than any other living diplomatic representative,
Was now a sort of warning to all diplomatic students
Of the risks attached to negligence, the perils of imprudence,
And, branded in the Honours List as 'Platypus, Dame Vera,'
Retired, a lonely figure, to lay eggs at Bordighera.

JOHN WILMOT, EARL OF ROCHESTER

Impromptu on Charles II

God bless our good and gracious King,
    Whose promise none relies on;
Who never said a foolish thing,
    Nor ever did a wise one.

On His Own Career

Few thought he was even a starter,
There were many who thought themselves smarter,
    But he ended PM,
    CH and OM,
An earl and a knight of the garter.

On a General Election

The accursed power which stands on Privilege
(And goes with Women, and Champagne and Bridge)
Broke – and Democracy resumed her reign:
(Which goes with Bridge, and Women and Champagne).

Managing the Common Herd:
two approaches for senior management

THEORY X: People are naturally lazy.
They come late, leave early, feign illness.
When they sit at their desks
it's ten to one they're yakking to colleagues
on the subject of who qualifies as a gorgeous hunk.
They're coating their lips and nails with slop,
a magazine open to 'What your nails say about you'
or 'Ten exercises to keep your bottom in top form'
under this year's annual report.
These people need punishment;
they require stern warnings
and threats – don't be a coward,
don't be intimidated by a batting eyelash.
Stand firm: a few tears, a Mars Bar,
several glasses of cider with her pals tonight
and you'll be just the same old
rat-bag, mealy-mouthed, small-minded tyrant
you were before you docked her
fifteen minutes pay for insubordination.

Never let these con-artists get the better of you.

THEORY Z: Staff need encouragement.
Give them a little responsibility
and watch their eager faces lighting up.
Let them know their input is important.
Be democratic – allow all of them
their two cents worth of gripes.
(Don't forget this is the Dr Spock generation.)

[123]

If eight out of twelve of them
prefer green garbage cans to black ones
under their desks, be generous –
the dividends in productivity
will be reaped with compound interest.
Offer incentives, show them
it's to their *own* advantage to meet targets.
Don't talk down to your employees.
Make staff believe that they
have valid and innovative ideas
and that not only are you interested,
but that you will act upon them.

Remember, they're human too.

GAVIN EWART

The Meeting

In the long and boring meeting,
in the hot and boring meeting,
there was shouting by the Chairman,
bullying almost by the Chairman,
people rose on points of order,
caused chaos with points of order,
argument became emotive,
all the words used were emotive,
and this was the obvious reason
passion overcame all reason.

Everything was twice repeated,
sometimes more than twice repeated,
as they worked through the agenda
(it seemed elastic, that agenda,
becoming longer, never shorter),
their utterances grew long, not shorter,
it was just like spreading butter,
words went further, like spread butter,
covering each subject thinly,
covering almost nothing thinly.

People talked about resigning,
disgruntled talk was of resigning,
accusations in a covey
flew like partridge in a covey,
yet this was not entertaining –
it sounds like drama, entertaining

as the TV scenes in courtrooms –
this was *not* like scenes in courtrooms,
it contrived to be quite boring,
really quite immensely boring.

It was more like scenes where children
shout insults at other children,
it was like a verbal punch-up,
more long-winded than a punch-up,
but the bitterness and anger
brought out words like knives in anger,
it was more like verbal murder
if there's boredom in a murder –
any moderate survivors
in the end *felt* like survivors.

Like being rescued from a snowstorm,
or blinding words whirled like a snowstorm;
they could only cry for brandy,
go to pubs and order brandy,
they felt they deserved some medals
like the Army's campaign medals –
through the tumult and the shouting
(quiet was strange after the shouting)
they achieved the peace of something
through the meeting – which was something.

It was like peace after beating
heads on walls, like hours of beating
heads on walls and never stopping –
till at last the joy of stopping
seemed a truly great achievement,
lack of pain, a great achievement,

it's so lovely when you stop it!
Negative delight, to stop it,
flooded through them after meeting
at that long hot boring meeting!

ANONYMOUS

Advice to Copywriters

When your client's hopping mad
Put his picture in the ad.
If he still should prove refractory
Add a picture of his factory.

Executive

I am a young executive. No cuffs than mine are cleaner;
I have a Slimline brief-case and I use the firm's Cortina.
In every roadside hostelry from here to Burgess Hill
The *maîtres d'hôtel* all know me well and let me sign the bill.

You ask me what it is I do. Well actually, you know,
I'm partly a liaison man and partly P.R.O.
Essentially I integrate the current export drive
And basically I'm viable from ten o'clock till five.

For vital off-the-record work – that's talking transport-
    wise –
I've a scarlet Aston-Martin – and does she go? She flies!
Pedestrians and dogs and cats – we mark them down for
    slaughter.
I also own a speed-boat which has never touched the water.

She's built of fibre-glass, of course. I call her 'Mandy Jane'
After a bird I used to know – No soda, please, just plain –
And how did I acquire her? Well to tell you about that
And to put you in the picture I must wear my other hat.

I do some mild developing. The sort of place I need
Is a quiet country market town that's rather run to seed.
A luncheon and a drink or two, a little *savoir faire* –
I fix the Planning Officer, the Town Clerk and the Mayor.

And if some preservationist attempts to interfere
A 'dangerous structure' notice from the Borough Engineer
Will settle any buildings that are standing in our way –
The modern style, sir, with respect, has really come to stay.

ANONYMOUS

Going to The Dogs

My granddad, viewing earth's worn cogs,
Said things were going to the dogs;
His granddad in his house of logs,
Said things were going to the dogs;
His granddad in the Flemish bogs,
Said things were going to the dogs;
His granddad in his old skin togs,
Said things were going to the dogs;
There's one thing that I have to state –
The dogs have had a good long wait.

I Was Fair Beat

I spent a nicht amang the cognoscenti,
a hie-brou clan, ilk wi a beard on him
like Mark Twain's miners, due to hae a trim,
their years on aiverage roun three-and-twenty.

Of poetry and music we had plenty,
owre muckle, but ye maun be in the swim:
Kurt Schwitters' Ur-sonata that gaes 'Grimm
glimm gnimm bimmbimm,' it fairly wad hae sent ye

daft, if ye'd been there; modern jazz wi juicy
snell wud-wind chords, three new yins, I heard say
by thaim that ken't, new, that is, sen Debussy.

Man, it was awfie. I wad raither hae
a serenata sung by randy pussy,
and what a time a reel of tape can play!

The James Bond Movie

The popcorn is greasy, and I forgot to bring a Kleenex.
A pill that's a bomb inside the stomach of a man inside

The Embassy blows up. Eructations of flame, luxurious
cauliflowers giganticize into motion. The entire 29-ft.

screen is orange, is crackling flesh and brick bursting,
blackening, smithereened. I unwrap a Dentyne and, while

jouncing my teeth in rubber tongue-smarting clove, try
with the 2-inch-wide paper to blot butter off my fingers.

A bubble-bath, room-sized, in which 14 girls, delectable,
and sexless, twist-topped Creamy Freezes (their blond,

red, brown, pinkish, lavender or silver wiglets all
screwed that high, and varnished), scrub-tickle a lone

male, whose chest has just the right amount and distribu-
tion of curly hair. He's nervously pretending to defend

his modesty. His crotch, below the waterline, is also
below the frame – but unsubmerged all 28 slick foamy
　　boobs.

Their make-up fails to let the girls look naked. Caterpil-
lar lashes, black and thick, lush lips glossed pink like

the gum I pop and chew, contact lenses on the eyes that are
mostly blue, they're nose-perfect replicas of each other.

I've got most of the grease off and onto this little square
of paper. I'm folding it now, making creases with my nails.

We Don't Need To Leave Yet, Do We?
or, Yes We Do

One kind of person when catching a train always wants to
allow an hour to cover the ten-block trip to the
terminus.

And the other kind looks at them as if they were
verminous,

And the second kind says that five minutes is plenty and
will even leave one minute over for buying the tickets,

And the first kind looks at them as if they had cerebral
rickets.

One kind when theater-bound sups lightly at six and
hastens off to the play,

And indeed I know one such person who is so such that it
frequently arrives in time for the last act of the matinée,

And the other kind sits down at eight to a meal that is
positively sumptuous,

Observing cynically that an eight-thirty curtain never
rises till eight-forty, an observation which is less
cynical than bumptuous.

And what the first kind, sitting uncomfortably in the
waiting room while the train is made up in the yards,
can never understand,

Is the injustice of the second kind's reaching their seat just
as the train moves out, just as they had planned,

And what the second kind cannot understand as they
stumble over the first kind's feet just as the footlights
flash on at last

Is that the first kind doesn't feel the least bit foolish at
having entered the theater before the cast.

Oh, the first kind always wants to start now and the
   second kind always wants to tarry,
Which wouldn't make any difference, except that each
   other is what they always marry.

How to Treat the House-Plants

All she ever thinks about are house-plants.
She talks to them and tends them every day.
And she says, 'Don't hurt their feelings. Give them
Love. In all your dealings with them,
Treat them in a tender, *human* way.'

'Certainly, my dear,' he says. 'OK.
Human, eh?'

But the house-plants do not seem to want to play.

They are stooping, they are drooping,
They are kneeling in their clay:
They are flaking, they are moulting,
Turning yellow, turning grey,
And they look . . . well, quite revolting
As they sigh, and fade away.

So after she has left the house he gets them
And he sets them in a line against the wall,
And I cannot say he cossets them or pets them –
No, he doesn't sympathize with them at all.
Is he tender? Is he human? Not a bit.
No, to each of them in turn he says: 'You *twit!*

You're a
    Rotten little skiver,
    Cost a fiver,
    Earn your keep!

You're a
    Dirty little drop-out!
    You're a cop-out!
    You're a creep!

You're a
    Mangy little whinger!
    You're a cringer!
    Son, it's true –

    I have justbin
    To the dustbin
    Where there's *better men than you*!

    Get that stem back!

    Pull your weight!

    Stick your leaves out!

    STAND UP STRAIGHT!'

And, strange to say, the plants co-operate.
So when she comes back home and finds them glowing,
Green and healthy, every one a king,
She says, 'It's *tenderness* that gets them growing!
How strange, the change a little *love* can bring!'

'Oh yes,' he says. 'Not half. Right. Love's the thing.'

Bunthorne's Song

(from Patience*)*

If you're anxious for to shine in the high aesthetic line as
 a man of culture rare,
You must get up all the germs of the transcendental terms,
 and plant them everywhere.
You must lie upon the daisies and discourse in novel
 phrases of your complicated state of mind.
The meaning doesn't matter if it's only idle chatter of a
 transcendental kind.
And every one will say,
As you walk your mystic way,
'If this young man expresses himself in terms too deep for *me*,
Why, what a very singularly deep young man this deep
 young man must be!'

Be eloquent in praise of the very dull old days which have
 long since passed away,
And convince 'em, if you can, that the reign of good Queen
 Anne was Culture's palmiest day.
Of course you will pooh-pooh whatever's fresh and new,
 and declare it's crude and mean,
For Art stopped short in the cultivated court of the Empress
 Josephine.
And every one will say,
As you walk your mystic way,
'If that's not good enough for him which is good enough
 for *me*,
Why, what a very cultivated kind of youth this kind of
 youth must be!'

Then a sentimental passion of a vegetable fashion must
    excite your languid spleen,
An attachment *à la Plato* for a bashful young potato, or a
    not-too-French French bean!
Though the Philistines may jostle, you will rank as an
    apostle in the high aesthetic band,
If you walk down Piccadilly with a poppy or a lily in your
    mediaeval hand.
And every one will say
As you walk your flowery way,
'If he's content with a vegetable love which would
    certainly not suit *me*,
Why, what a most particularly pure young man this pure
    young man must be!'

PAUL DURCAN

Raymond of the Rooftops

The morning after the night
The roof flew off the house
And our sleeping children narrowly missed
Being decapitated by falling slates,
I asked my husband if he would
Help me put back the roof:
But no – he was too busy at his work
Writing for a women's magazine in London
An Irish Fairytale called *Raymond of the Rooftops*.
Will you have a heart, woman – he bellowed –
Can't you see I am up to my eyes and ears in work,
Breaking my neck to finish *Raymond of the Rooftops*,
Fighting against time to finish *Raymond of the Rooftops*,
Putting everything I have got into *Raymond of the Rooftops*?

Isn't it well for him? *Everything he has got!*

All I wanted him to do was to stand
For an hour, maybe two hours, three at the most,
At the bottom of the stepladder
And hand me up slates while I slated the roof:
But no – once again I was proving to be the insensitive,
Thoughtless, feckless even, wife of the artist.
There was I up to my fat, raw knees in rainwater
Worrying him about the hole in our roof
While he was up to his neck in *Raymond of the Rooftops*.
Will you have a heart, woman – he bellowed –
Can't you see I am up to my eyes and ears in work,
Breaking my neck to finish *Raymond of the Rooftops*,

Fighting against time to finish *Raymond of the Rooftops*,
Putting everything I have got into *Raymond of the Rooftops*?

Isn't it well for him? *Everything he has got!*

Celtic

The Irish are great talkers,
persuasive and disarming.
You can say lots and lots
against the Scots –
but at least they're never charming!

This Englishwoman

This Englishwoman is so refined
She has no bosom and no behind.

Out of Africa

Out of Africa of the suckling
Out of Africa of the tired woman in earrings
Out of Africa of the black-foot leap
Out of Africa of the baobab, the suck-teeth
Out of Africa of the dry maw of hunger
Out of Africa of the first rains, the first mother.

Into the Caribbean of the staggeringly blue sea-eye
Into the Caribbean of the baleful tourist glare
Into the Caribbean of the hurricane
Into the Caribbean of the flame tree, the palm tree,
the ackee, the high smelling saltfish
and the happy creole so-called mentality.

Into England of the frost and the tea
Into England of the budgie and the strawberry
Into England of the trampled autumn tongues
Into England of the meagre funerals
Into England of the hand of the old woman
And the gent running behind someone
who's forgotten their umbrella, crying out,
'I say . . . I say-ay.'

Welsh Incident

'But that was nothing to what things came out
From the sea-caves of Criccieth yonder.'
'What were they? Mermaids? dragons? ghosts?'
'Nothing at all of any things like that.'
'What were they, then?'
                                    'All sorts of queer things,
Things never seen or heard or written about,
Very strange, un-Welsh, utterly peculiar
Things. Oh, solid enough they seemed to touch,
Had anyone dared it. Marvellous creation,
All various shapes and sizes, and no sizes,
All new, each perfectly unlike his neighbour,
Though all came moving slowly out together.'
'Describe just one of them.'
                                    'I am unable.'
'What were their colours?'
                                    'Mostly nameless colours,
Colours you'd like to see; but one was puce
Or perhaps more like crimson, but not purplish.
Some had no colour.'
                                    'Tell me, had they legs?'
'Not a leg nor foot among them that I saw.'
'But did these things come out in any order?
What o'clock was it? What was the day of the week?
Who else was present? How was the weather?
'I was coming to that. It was half-past three
On Easter Tuesday last. The sun was shining.
The Harlech Silver Band played *Marchog Jesu*
On thirty-seven shimmering instruments,

Collecting for Caernarvon's (Fever) Hospital Fund.
The populations of Pwllheli, Criccieth,
Portmadoc, Borth, Tremadoc, Penrhyndeudraeth,
Were all assembled. Criccieth's mayor addressed them
First in good Welsh and then in fluent English,
Twisting his fingers in his chain of office,
Welcoming the things. They came out on the sand,
Not keeping time to the band, moving seaward
Silently at a snail's pace. But at last
The most odd, indescribable thing of all,
Which hardly one man there could see for wonder,
Did something recognizably a something.'
'Well, what?'
              'It made a noise.'
                              'A frightening noise?'
'No, no.'
        'A musical noise? A noise of scuffling?'
'No, but a very loud, respectable noise –
Like groaning to oneself on Sunday morning
In Chapel, close before the second psalm.'
'What did the mayor do?'
                        'I was coming to that.'

MARTYN WILEY and IAN MCMILLAN

Three Riddled Riddles

(i)

I have nine legs.
I carry an umbrella.
I live in a box
at the bottom of a ship.
At night
I play the trombone.

What am I?

Answer: I've forgotten.

(ii)

You see me at dawn
with the clouds in my hair.
I run like a horse
and sing like a nightingale.
I collect stamps
and coconuts.

What am I?

Answer: I'm not sure.

(iii)

I taste like a grapefruit.
I swim like a chair.
I hang on the trees
and people tap my face,

rake my soil
and tell me jokes.

What am I?

Answer: I've really no idea.

CHRISTOPHER REID

By the By

Through a helpful warder,
I soon met the legendary
Dr Spillaine,
author of the *Contradictionary* –
that vast rebuttal
of all established
lexicographical lore.
There was hardly a word
whose accepted meaning
he had not contested
and the whole enterprise rested
on his glorious disdain
for so-called alphabetical order.

The Mad Gardener's Song

He thought he saw an Elephant,
   That practised on a fife:
He looked again, and found it was
   A letter from his wife.
'At length I realise,' he said,
   'The bitterness of Life!'

He thought he saw a Buffalo
   Upon the chimney-piece:
He looked again, and found it was
   His Sister's Husband's Niece.
'Unless you leave this house,' he said,
   'I'll send for the Police!'

He thought he saw a Rattlesnake
   That questioned him in Greek:
He looked again, and found it was
   The Middle of Next Week.
'The one thing I regret,' he said,
   'Is that it cannot speak!'

He thought he saw a Banker's Clerk
   Descending from the bus:
He looked again, and found it was
   A Hippopotamus:
'If this should stay to dine,' he said,
   'There won't be much for us!'

He thought he saw a Kangaroo
    That worked a coffee-mill:
He looked again, and found it was
    A Vegetable-Pill.
'Were I to swallow this,' he said,
    'I should be very ill!'

He thought he saw a Coach-and-Four
    That stood beside his bed:
He looked again, and found it was
    A Bear without a Head.
'Poor thing,' he said, 'poor silly thing!'
    'It's waiting to be fed!'

He thought he saw an Albatross
    That fluttered round the lamp:
He looked again, and found it was
    A Penny-Postage-Stamp.
'You'd best be getting home,' he said:
    'The nights are very damp!'

He thought he saw a Garden-Door
    That opened with a key:
He looked again, and found it was
    A Double Rule of Three:
'And all its mystery,' he said,
    'Is clear as day to me!'

He thought he saw an Argument
    That proved he was the Pope:
He looked again and found it was
    A Bar of Mottled Soap.
'A fact so dread,' he faintly said,
    'Extinguishes all hope!'

Acknowledgements

The editor and publishers gratefully acknowledge permission to reprint copyright material in this book as follows:

FLEUR ADCOCK: 'Things' from *Selected Poems* (1983) reprinted by permission of Oxford University Press. JOHN AGARD: 'On First-Name Terms' from *The Devil's Pulpit* (Bloodaxe) by permission of Bloodaxe Books Ltd. SIMON ARMITAGE: 'Very Simply Topping Up the Brake Fluid' from *Zoom!* (Bloodaxe) by permission of Bloodaxe Books Ltd. W. H. AUDEN: Faber and Faber Ltd for 'On the Circuit' and 'from Shorts' from *Collected Poems*, edited by Edward Mendelson (1976). HILAIRE BELLOC: 'On a General Election' and 'Fatigue' from *Complete Verse* (Pimlico) reprinted by permission of the Peters Fraser and Dunlop Group Limited on behalf of the Estate of Hilaire Belloc. CONNIE BENSLEY: 'Mr and Mrs R and the Christmas Card List' from *Choosing To Be a Swan* (Bloodaxe) by permission of Bloodaxe Books Ltd. JOHN BETJEMAN: 'Executive' from *Collected Poems* (John Murray, Publishers, Ltd) by permission of Desmond Elliott, the Administrator of the Estate. G. K. CHESTERTON: 'Ballade of Suicide' and 'A Ballad of Appreciation' by permission of A. P. Watt Ltd on behalf of the Royal Literary Fund. WENDY COPE: Faber and Faber Ltd for 'Strugnell's Haiku' from *Making Cocoa for Kingsley Amis*. WALTER DE LA MARE: 'The Bards' from *Complete Poems of Walter de la Mare* (Faber and Faber, 1969) by permission of the Literary Trustees of Walter de la Mare and the Society of Authors as their representative. IAN DUHIG: 'Margin Prayer from an Ancient Psalter' from *The Bradford Count* (Bloodaxe) by permission of Bloodaxe Books Ltd. DOUGLAS DUNN: Faber and Faber Ltd for 'Extra Helpings' from *Dante's Drum-Kit*. PAUL DURCAN: 'Raymond of the Rooftops' by kind permission of the author. D. J. ENRIGHT: Extracts from 'Paradise Illustrated' from *Collected Poems* (OUP) by permission of the author, Oxford University Press and Watson, Little Ltd as licensing agents. JAMES FENTON: 'The Skip' from *Out of Danger*, reprinted by permission of Penguin Books Ltd. ROBERT GARIOCH: 'I was Fair Beat' by permission of the Saltire Society. ROBERT GRAVES: 'Welsh Incident' from *Collected Poems* by permission of Carcanet Press Limited.

Index of Poets

Index of First Lines